LETTS POCKET GUIDE TO

BIRDS

Nearly 200 of the most common British
birds described and illustrated in colour

Mike Lambert and Alan Pearson

CHARLES LETTS
Letts
of London®
FOUNDED 1796

Front cover illustration: Coal Tits

This edition first published 1990
by Charles Letts & Co Ltd
Letts of London House,
Parkgate Road,
London SW11 4NQ

'Letts' is a registered trademark of
Charles Letts & Co Limited

This edition produced under licence by
Malcolm Saunders Publishing Ltd, London

© 1990 this edition Atlantis Publications Ltd

© 1990 text and illustrations A. Pearson & M. Lambert

Reprinted 1991, 1993

A CIP Catalogue record for this book is available
from the British Library

ISBN 1 85238 101 9

Printed in Spain by Graficas Reunidas

Contents

Introduction

The chief aim of this book is to enable the reader, and newcomer to birdwatching, to identify positively and as simply as possible the great majority of birds which he is likely to encounter.

We all come into contact with birds, most of us with more interest and curiosity than specialist knowledge. This simple pocket-sized guide will enable you to identify a bird seen on a country walk, on holiday, or a visitor to the back garden, and will add to the casual observer's knowledge of common bird species.

There is, to be sure, no shortage of books on birds, but most of them group birds in families which makes identification a confusing and time-consuming process. A bird is unlikely to wait around and pose helpfully while the enthusiastic beginner leafs through an entire list of birds in the hope of identifying the species before him. If he has little or no idea which family a particular bird might belong to, where is he to begin?

Similarly, it is often difficult to establish from traditional guides whether a bird is a real rarity or merely a little uncommon. Thus it would be a simple error to decide that a small thin-billed greenish little bird was a Greenish Warbler, when it was in fact the far more common Willow Warbler.

Letts Pocket Guide to Birds avoids confusion by editing out rarities such as the Greenish Warbler. Only the most common species have been featured and it is worth stressing that these are not necessarily the most common in terms of numbers, but those that the non-expert beginner is most likely to meet. So birds that are shy of humans or that are found only in inaccessible regions have been omitted, since they are only rarely seen.

So you will not have to go out of your way to see any of the birds featured here and with the help of this simple identification guide you will, we hope, increase and expand your interest and knowledge.

Most of the more unusual species are listed in group colour plates in the Less common species section (pp 118-125). If you regularly see species from this additional selection, then you have probably outgrown this book and should seek more specialist guides.

How to use this book

To enable the newcomer to birdwatching to make a positive identification as simply as possible, we have divided the birds into sections according to the type of location where you are most likely to see them.

If, for instance, you want to identify a bird seen on a walk in the woods, you should consult the section headed **Birds of town, garden, park and woodland**. Each section, that is each type of habitat, is clearly distinguished by the different coloured bands at the top of the page (see Fig 1).

Within each of these sections, birds are not ordered by family but by size, since it is grouping by family that makes most bird guides so difficult for beginners to follow. So, knowing where you saw the bird and having turned to the appropriate section, you need to make a rough guess at its size.

How big was the bird?

Birds are featured in order of size from smallest to largest and the relative size category is denoted by a symbol at the top of each page beside the name of the bird (see Fig 2). This means that two birds of the same family may be separated by a bird or birds of intermediate size. For example, two of the commonest Woodpeckers will be found as follows: Great Spotted at 23cm (9in) and Green Woodpecker at 32cm (12-13in).

Fig 1. Locating the bird

Birds of town, garden, park and woodland

Birds of farmland, open moor, inland waterways and wild country

Birds of estuary, coast and sea

Less common species

Fig 2 Guide to bird sizes
All sizes refer to the length of the bird, from bill-tip to tail-end.

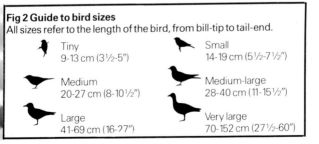

Tiny
9-13 cm (3½-5")

Small
14-19 cm (5½-7½")

Medium
20-27 cm (8-10½")

Medium-large
28-40 cm (11-15½")

Large
41-69 cm (16-27")

Very large
70-152 cm (27½-60")

By flicking through the book you have quickly narrowed the field down to birds of a particular size in a particular location. The information you need to make a positive identification is contained in the coloured boxes beneath the illustration of each bird. A specimen page is shown in Fig 3.

Distinguishing marks

The first box describes the feature or combination of features that are unique to that bird of that size range. In other words, if you are certain of these features, which are also borne out by the colour illustration, you have already *positively identified* the bird and need read on only out of interest and to build up a more detailed picture of it.

If you are uncertain about these specific features, then the second box completes the description. The third box adds localities and typical habits. However, the second and third boxes, although they provide additional information, do not specifically identify the particular bird. Only the first box can do that.

The fourth box on each page gives the names of similar birds with which the featured bird could be confused. All these 'Lookalikes' are either featured in detail themselves or appear under the heading of **Less common species** in section 4. The names and features of less common birds are given in brackets, so if you turn to page 37, *Collared Dove,* you will see its lookalikes listed as *(Turtle Dove: . . .) Feral Pigeon* and *Wood Pigeon.* This means that the Feral and Wood Pigeon are featured in sections 1-3, while the Turtle Dove is to be found under **Less common species.**

Lookalikes

This Lookalikes box is important for two reasons. Firstly it is all too easy to jump to conclusions when looking for known identifying features. You can, in effect, already have made up your mind about the bird's identity before checking its specific features in the top box. Check the Lookalikes carefully. Size is easily misjudged and buff plumage, for instance, often mistaken for yellow. This box will give you other possibilities to consider.

Secondly, it is very important for the observer to be aware of exactly what points he should be looking for, as a means of quickly distinguishing similar birds. This is where guesswork ends and skill begins.

After the three sections of birds featured individually according to typical habitat, section 4 is a grouping, again in strictly size order, of other species which are likely to be observed by non-experts. No text accompanies the illustrations, just the name and size of each species, with its distinguishing features pinpointed.

Before you set out, it is worth emphasising that birds are not glued to their habitat and may travel widely. The habitat divisions in this book indicate the most likely location for each bird. But be prepared to consider information on localities and habits in the third box, if you feel sure that you have seen a bird out of habitat. Any usual variations will be listed.

Suddenly a bird is disturbed in front of you. How big was it? Always err slightly on the small size. If you think it was the size of a Blackbird (25cm or 10in), start with the 22cm (8-9in) long birds and progress through the pages until you see the one that looks similar. Check the first box containing the specific features. If it tallies with what you have seen, you have identified the bird from a minimum of detail. The second, third and Lookalike boxes should reinforce your identification and also make you aware of similar birds with different specific features.

Good birdwatching, and don't forget to tick off your sightings on the check-list provided with the index!

Fig. 3. Specimen Page

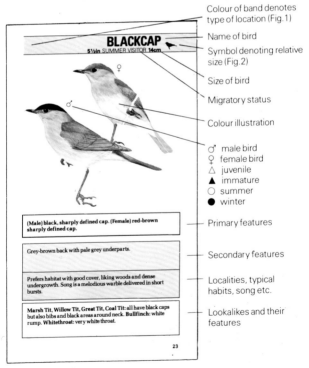

Colour of band denotes type of location (Fig.1)

Name of bird

Symbol denoting relative size (Fig.2)

Size of bird

Migratory status

Colour illustration

♂ male bird
♀ female bird
△ juvenile
▲ immature
○ summer
● winter

Primary features

Secondary features

Localities, typical habits, song etc.

Lookalikes and their features

Within the illustration:

BLACKCAP
5½in SUMMER VISITOR 14cm

♀

♂

(Male) black, sharply defined cap. (Female) red-brown sharply defined cap.

Grey-brown back with pale grey underparts.

Prefers habitat with good cover, liking woods and dense undergrowth. Song is a melodious warble delivered in short bursts.

Marsh Tit, Willow Tit, Great Tit, Coal Tit: all have black caps but also bibs and black areas around neck. Bullfinch: white rump. Whitethroat: very white throat.

23

Glossary of terms

Adult A mature bird capable of breeding.

Bib A distinctively coloured patch of feathers in the throat and upper breast region, e.g. Coal Tit.

Call-note A few notes, or even a single note, indicating alarm or acting as a simple statement of presence.

Decurved Curved downwards, e.g. the bill of the Curlew.

Display A ritualised pattern of behaviour, usually movement, by which birds communicate with each other, particularly during courtship and in defence of territory.

Female Otherwise known as the hen (general), duck (ducks), goose (geese) or pen (swans).

Feral Established in a wild state but originating from domesticated stock.

Immature A fully grown bird but not yet old enough to breed; immature plumage may be distinctively different from adult.

Juvenile A young bird in its own first plumage variation, having left the nest but not yet completed its first moult at the end of the summer.

Male Otherwise known as the cock (general), drake (ducks), gander (geese) or cob (swans).

Mask A distinctively coloured patch of feathers on the cheek and around the eyes, often joined, if only thinly, across the forehead, e.g. Lesser Whitethroat.

Passage migrant A migratory species, usually seen briefly in spring and or autumn, en route to its breeding or wintering grounds, e.g. Knot.

Resident Present throughout the year, e.g. Blackbird; the resident population may be supplemented at certain times of the year by individuals from abroad, e.g. Starling.

Shield A structure, lacking feathers, on the forehead of some waterbirds, e.g. Coot.

Song A sustained and consistent collection of notes, a trill or a warble, used principally to proclaim ownership of territory, particularly during the breeding season.

Spatulate Having a long, spread and flattened shape, e.g. the bill of the Shoveler.

Species A group of individuals (population) whose members resemble each other more closely than they resemble members of other populations and which, almost invariably, are capable of breeding only amongst themselves.

Speculum A panel on the trailing edge of the inner wing feathers of ducks, usually highly and distinctively coloured.

Sub-species A group of individuals within a species which differ slightly, usually in plumage, from the typical form but which are capable of breeding with any individual of that species.

Summer visitor A migratory species, arriving in spring and returning to its winter home at the end of the breeding season, e.g. Swallow.

Tube-nosed Having nostrils in the form of slightly raised tubes running forwards from the extreme base of the bill, e.g. Fulmar.

Wing-bar A relatively narrow band of colour along the length of the wing, e.g. Chaffinch.

Wing flash A relatively narrow band of colour across the width of the wing, e.g. Wood Pigeon.

Wing patch A relatively large area of colour on the wing, e.g. Greenfinch.

Winter visitor A migratory species, arriving in late autumn and returning to its summer home to breed when conditions there improve in spring, e.g. Redwing.

Fig 4. The parts of a bird

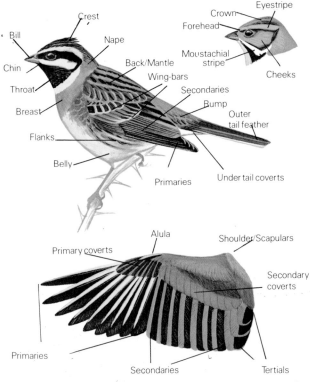

GOLDCREST
9cm RESIDENT **3½in**

Tiny bird with yellow crown edged with black.

Plump, active bird with olive-green back and off-white underparts. Two white wing-bars.

Prefers coniferous woodlands, sometimes in evergreen hedges and bushes in gardens. Actively searches for small insects mainly in the higher branches. Not shy of man.

(**Firecrest:** almost identical; prominent white stripe between black edge of crown and eye.) **Warblers** and **tits:** beware – similar size and flitting, foraging behaviour may confuse, especially high in the trees. However, markings of Goldcrest are distinctive.

Tiny brown bird with upright tail.

Brown plumage closely barred, darker above and paler below. Distinctive, straight, rapid flight on whirring wings, and surprisingly powerful song.

One of our commonest birds and it is found mostly in areas with dense, low cover. Particularly favours ivy thickets in which to build its domed nest.

None.

11

No wing-bars and (April-July) musical song consisting of descending sequence of notes ending in a flourish.

Pale eye-stripe and olive-green back. Intensity of yellow underparts varies according to individual and season. Paler belly. Legs generally light-brown but very variable. Call (not song) repeated di-syllabic 'hoo-eet'.

Commons, heaths and lightly wooded land are preferred habitat for this numerous summer visitor.

Chiffchaff: so similar that most observers call both 'Willow-Chiffs'; song: distinctive, repeated 'chiffchaff', and call: single-syllable 'hweet'; legs generally dark. (**Wood Warbler:** yellow-green back; bright yellow breast; white belly; prefers woods.)

CHIFFCHAFF
4½in SUMMER VISITOR 11cm

No wing-bars. Song is a repeated 'chiffchaff, chiffchaff'.

Pale eye-stripe and olive-green back. Underparts yellow, varying in intensity according to individual and season. Belly paler. Legs usually dark. Call (as opposed to song) is a one-syllable 'hweet'.

Inhabits woods and thick undergrowth.

Willow Warbler: so similar that most observers are content to call both 'Willow-Chiffs'; generally legs paler brown and colours slightly brighter; song: distinctive, prolonged, musical warble; call: di-syllabic 'hoo-eet'. **(Wood Warbler:** yellow-green back; bright yellow breast; white belly.)

White patch on nape and buff belly.

Glossy black crown and white cheeks. Two white wing-bars and olive-grey back.

The smallest tit, inhabits woods and gardens. Very common, often flocking with other tit species.

Great Tit: much larger; yellow belly with prominent black stripe; green back. **Marsh** and **Willow Tits:** lack white nape and white wing-bars. **Blue Tit:** blue crown and yellow belly.

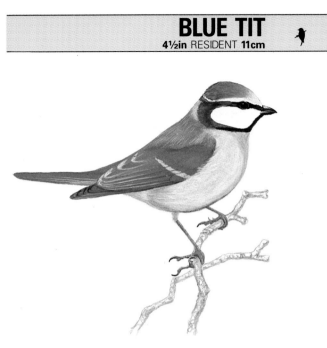

Blue crown and yellow belly.

Blue wings and tail. Fine stripe down belly. White cheeks and border to blue crown. Green back.

Extremely acrobatic in searching for insects on twigs and branches. Very common in woods, gardens and hedgerows; often flocks with other tits.

Great Tit: larger; black crown; white cheeks; prominent black stripe down belly. **Coal Tit:** black crown; white nape; lacks stripe on buff belly.

15

Glossy black cap and no wing-bars or pale patch on wing.

Brown back. Off-white cheeks and underparts. Small black bib.

Woodland bird, preferring deciduous trees. Typical tit, flitting along branches seeking insects.

Willow Tit: almost identical but has dull cap and pale patch on inner wing. **Coal Tit:** white patch on nape; buff belly. **Blackcap** (male): grey back; lacks black bib.

Dull black cap and light patch on inner wing.

Brown back, off-white cheeks and underparts. Small black bib.

Despite name, prefers wet woodlands and marshy areas with trees, though often occurs with Marsh Tit which generally favours drier habitats.

Marsh Tit: almost identical but has glossy cap and lacks light patch on inner wing. **Coal Tit:** white patch on nape; buff belly. **Blackcap** (male): grey back; lacks black bib.

Reminiscent of a Swallow but with white rump.

Blue-black crown, back, wings and forked tail. White underparts. White feathered legs.

Common around buildings but also in open country. Like others of the Swallow family, usually seen on the wing in pursuit of insects. May settle on the ground, particularly to collect mud to build a nest under the eaves of a house.

Swallow: long, forked tail; red face. **Sand Martin:** brown back and band on breast; lacks white rump. **Swift:** scythe-like wings; almost completely brown-black.

Downward-curved bill.

Small, active, mouse-like bird. Brown with white underparts, white eye-stripe and buff wing-bars.

Aptly named, usually seen climbing tree trunks in search of insects using stiff tail feathers as a support, like a Woodpecker. Motion is jerky and only rarely descends trees. Primarily a woodland bird though may visit garden trees.

None.

NUTHATCH
14cm RESIDENT **5½in**

Able to climb on tree trunks in any direction.

Distinctive plumage with blue-grey crown, back and tail, pale buff underparts, chestnut flanks and prominent black eye-stripe.

Small, stumpy-tailed bird with awkward, jerky flight, usually confined to short distances between trees. Found in deciduous woodland and gardens where it finds and hoards nuts, acorns and insects.

None.

Mainly black and white with some pink plumage and very long, 7.5cm (3in) tail.

Black crown with white stripe in centre. Face and breast white. Belly, flanks, rump and mid-back pink. Wings and tail black edged with white.

Inhabits woodlands and hedgerows. Restless, acrobatic bird, often flocking with other tits.

Pied Wagtail: lacks pink plumage; generally seen feeding on the ground in open country; runs in a series of stops and starts.

Bright orange-red plumage from forehead to breast.

Green-brown above with pale grey margin around forehead and breast, shading to buff below.

Melodic warbling song usually given from prominent perch. Very common in gardens and woods. Despite 'friendly' nature suggested by their bold attitude to people, they are very aggressive in defending territories from each other.

Redstart: orange brown tail, frequently flicked upwards.

(Male) black, sharply defined cap. (Female) red-brown sharply defined cap.

Grey-brown back with pale grey underparts.

Prefers habitat with good cover, liking woods and dense undergrowth. Song is a melodious warble delivered in short bursts.

Marsh Tit, Willow Tit, Great Tit, Coal Tit: all have black caps but also bibs and black areas around neck. **Bullfinch:** white rump. **Whitethroat:** very white throat.

23

REDSTART
14cm SUMMER VISITOR **5½in**

Orange-brown tail which flicks frequently upwards. Male has white forehead. Female has buff underparts.

Male has black face and throat with orange-red underparts and a grey back. Female is nondescript with grey-brown upper parts.

An active restless bird whose short, fluttering flights and general behaviour are reminiscent of the Robin. Though widespread on heaths and in woodlands it is patchily distributed and easily overlooked.

(**Black Redstart:** (male) no white forehead or orange-red underparts; (female) darker and greyer.) **Robin:** no black face or white forehead. **Stonechat:** (male) white neck-patch on black head; (female) darker, white wing-patches, dark tail. (**Nightingale:** larger; skulking; liquid song.)

Brown bird, paler below and darker above, with unique lack of wing or tail markings and no eye-stripe.

This very nondescript bird is characterised by its lack of features. Slightly plumper than similar warblers with a pleasing, gentle expression. Tail square-ended.

Found in both woodland and open heath, its sustained warbling song often betrays its presence.

Reed Warbler: more slender; rounded tail; prefers marshy habitat. **Willow Warbler** and **Chiffchaff:** distinct eye-stripe. **Whitethroat:** very white throat; rufous wings.

SPOTTED FLYCATCHER
14cm SUMMER VISITOR **5½in**

Flycatching behaviour and streaked (not spotted) breast.

Unobtrusively marked. Light grey-brown back and tail, and pale breast. Brown streaks on crown, forehead and breast.

Preys on insects from a post or other prominent place. Darts from perch, twisting and turning acrobatically to catch an insect before returning to same perch. Found from April-September in woodland and large gardens.

Warblers: similarly slender with nondescript plumage only distinguishable on close view. Lacks the unmistakable flycatching behaviour.

Black stripe down belly (broader in male).

Yellow belly. White cheeks. Black bib typical of tits. Sexes similar.

Largest of the tit family. Very common. Frequents woods, gardens and hedgerows. Often flocks with other tits outside breeding season.

Blue Tit: much smaller; blue crown, wings and tail; fine, blue belly stripe. **Coal Tit:** smaller; prominent white nape; white cheeks; black crown; buff belly without stripe.

Olive-green plumage with bright yellow patches on wing.

Adults of both sexes have yellow-green rump and yellow patches on tail. Females and juveniles duller than male and juveniles show strong streaks above and below.

Frequents gardens and open farmland.

(**Siskin:** smaller; male has black crown, female strongly streaked below.) **Goldfinch:** distinctive yellow wing-bars; confusion unlikely except at long range.

HOUSE SPARROW

5¾in RESIDENT 15cm

Male has grey crown with a black bib. Female is nondescript with pale eye-stripe. Usually in close association with male.

Male has brown back streaked with black; brown nape and pale grey cheeks and white wing-bar. Grey rump and pale grey underparts. Female has duller brown back than male, but is also streaked.

Well known for its tameness in towns, but also common on farmland, often in flocks and in association with finches. Both sparrows and finches have deep bills typical of birds which eat grain.

Tree Sparrow: chocolate-brown crown with black cheek spots; white collar. **Dunnock:** (often called Hedge Sparrow) very different build; slender bill; no pale cheeks.

Grey head markings and underparts with a slender bill.

Brown back streaked black as the two true sparrows. The Dunnock is often misnamed Hedge Sparrow.

Shy, even skulking manner. Plump Robin-like build and delicate flight are totally distinctive. A solitary bird, it is normally found on the ground under bushes, hedgerows, etc.

House Sparrow: grey crown; black bib. **Tree Sparrow:** chocolate-brown crown; black spot on cheek.

Narrow scythe-like wings.

Uniformly brown-black swallow-like bird with small white throat patch. Tail is forked but without streamers.

Totally aerial except during the breeding season, at the nest, and if exhausted, in which case weak legs and long wings prevent take-off from the ground and bird usually dies. Flight is rapid and jerky in pursuit of prey.

Swallow: pale underparts, red face; (in adult) tail streamers.
House Martin: pale underparts and white rump. **Sand Martin:** pale underparts; brown bar on breast.

31

Δ

Spangled body plumage, which in summer is irridescent, and in winter is white-speckled.

Plump bodied with short, pointed wings. Juveniles initially are uniform mouse-brown, progressing to adult plumage.

May fly large distances daily in immense flocks. Famed for remarkable ability to mimic other birds' songs in addition to its own guttural warbles and whistles.

None.

Pied plumage with prominent white shoulder patches.

Black crown, white cheeks, crimson on nape (male only) and under tail. Black back, white shoulders, and barred white-on-black wings give striking pied effect in flight. Underparts buff-white.

Widespread in mixed woodland, parks and secluded gardens. Loud, fast 'drumming' with bill on trees. Flight highly undulating.

(**Lesser Spotted Woodpecker:** much smaller (Sparrow-sized); white bars instead of patches on shoulder; crimson head (male only).)

SONG THRUSH
23cm RESIDENT **9in**

Typical thrush with speckled breast and orange underwing.

Warm brown back and head.

Common garden bird with direct flight. Often seen cracking snail shells open on stones. Builds a mud-lined nest in garden hedgerows for its sky-blue and black spotted eggs.

Mistle Thrush: larger; head greyer; white underwing and outer tail feathers. **Redwing:** smaller; white eye-stripe; red flanks and underwing. **Fieldfare:** grey head; brown back; grey rump; white underwing.

The male is a uniformly black garden bird; while the female is uniformly brown.

Male has yellow bill and eye-rings. Female has light speckling on the breast and yellow eye-rings.

Probably Britain's commonest garden bird, found in gardens everywhere. Formerly common in ancestral, woodland habitat.

(**Ring Ouzel:** white gorget or band across upper breast.)

35

Thrush with grey-brown head and white outer tail feathers.

Typical speckled breast, with greyish brown back and head. White underwing.

Usually seen on playing fields and parks but also common in wooded areas. Less common in gardens. Country name 'Stormcock' from its habit of singing from a high perch in blustery or stormy conditions.

Song Thrush: smaller, orange underwing; browner back.
Redwing: smaller; white eye-stripe; red flanks and underwing.
Fieldfare: grey head; brown back; grey rump.

COLLARED DOVE

12½in RESIDENT **32cm**

Zig-zag collar markings.

A grey-brown backed dove with blue-grey wings. Broad white band on tail shows especially when alighting. Black collar is edged with white.

Most usually seen in parks and wooded gardens; also in larger flocks on smallholdings and farmland.

(**Turtle Dove**: orange-brown back feathers with black centres; pied patch on neck.) **Feral Pigeon:** no black and white collar. **Wood Pigeon:** green and white patches on neck; white flashes on wing.

GREEN WOODPECKER
30-33cm RESIDENT **12-13in**

Green with crimson crown.

A very distinctive bird. Yellow rump contrasts with green in unmistakable, undulating flight. Pale underparts and black patch on face.

Makes loud tapping rather than loud drumming of Spotted Woodpeckers. Its nickname 'Yaffle' comes from its loud, laughing call. Feeds mainly on the ground in deciduous woods, parks and gardens.

None.

FERAL PIGEON
13in RESIDENT **33cm**

Town pigeons with a fast direct flight and 'oor-coo-coo' call.

Plumage very variable. Those most like wild ancestors are grey with white rump and two large black wing bars. Other common varieties are black, brown and white or mottled grey, often without the white rump. Wings long and pointed.

May form large flocks in towns and on farmland where damage to crops may result. Their large, messy nests are a common sight on buildings and statues. Probably derived from domesticated Rock Doves.

Stock Dove: pinkish throat and breast; no black borders on underwing. **Wood Pigeon:** white flashes on wing; white neck-patch; pink breast. **Collared Dove:** white band on tail; zig-zag mark on neck. (**Turtle Dove:** white tail-band; pied neck markings.)

JACKDAW
33cm RESIDENT **13in**

Grey nape.

This black bird is frequently confused with the larger crows and rooks, despite clear grey nape and unmistakable call-note, a ringing 'chack'.

Favours woods and buildings, but also frequents sea and inland cliffs where nesting holes can be found. According to legend jackdaws love to steal bright objects.

Carrion Crow: larger; all black. **Rook:** larger with pale grey face.

BLACK-HEADED GULL

14-15in RESIDENT **35-38cm**

In summer has chocolate brown head and in winter has dark ear spots and red legs.

Red bill and legs (may fade to orange in winter); grey back and upper wings with broad white leading edge and black tips. Immatures and juveniles show varying amounts of brown on upper parts and black tip to the tail.

Common on coasts. Most widespread of gulls inland.

(Winter) **Common Gull:** yellow bill and legs; no ear spot. **Herring Gull:** flesh-coloured legs; no ear spot. **Kittiwake:** no white on wing tip; black legs. (Summer) **Arctic Tern** and **Common Tern:** black capped; forked tail.

Bright blue wing-patches with black bands.

White rump most conspicuous as bird flies away; wings black and white above with blue patch on coverts; body mainly pink; head has black and white crest and dark moustache-like streak.

Very shy and wary, it is most likely to be seen in slow and clumsy flight: Fond of woodland, it is agile in trees and may hop on ground. The most colourful of the crow family.

None.

Distinctive hooting call and flight call. Very large head in proportion to body.

Mottled brown back and upper wings; underparts and underwings buff streaked with brown. Mid-upper wing (scapulars) has white spots. Large black eyes, no ear tufts and short broad rounded wings.

Entirely nocturnal. Only flies by day when disturbed. Only in woodlands. Song is the 'hoo-hoo-hoo---hooooo' of the storybook owl. Flight-call a distinctive 'ker-wick'.

(**Short-eared Owl**: flies by day; pale underwing with black carpal (midwing) patches.) **Barn Owl**: pale or white face and underwing.

Pale grey back and yellow legs.

Slim gull with white head, belly, underwings and tail. Black wing ends with white tips and lightweight bill with no red spot. Streaked neck in winter. Immatures and juveniles show varying degrees of brown on back.

Coastal as other gulls and also inland, particularly on park and arable land. Not in fact the most common Gull.

Herring Gull: larger; heavier bill with red spot; flesh-coloured legs. **Black-headed Gull:** (winter) black ear spot; red bill and legs; broad white leading edge to wing. **Kittiwake:** no white on wing tips; black legs. **Fulmar:** straight wings without black tips; tubelike nostrils.

White wing-flashes and neck patch.

Our largest pigeon. Grey back and inner wing; blue-grey head rump and belly; outer wing and tail tip black; green patch next to white neck patch; pinkish breast. From below white band across middle of black tail.

Generally frequents woods, though also gardens and farmland (where large flocks may gather). Takes flight noisily when disturbed. Flight is fast and direct, but when displaying climbs steeply to glide down on V-shaped wings.

Stock Dove, Feral Pigeon; lack white wing-flashes and neck patch. **Collared Dove;** lacks white wing-patches, has zig-zag neck marking. (**Turtle Dove;** lacks white wing-flashes, has pied neck markings.)

Pied plumage with exceptionally long, wedge-ended tail.

Black plumage is actually dark blue and dark green in parts. Otherwise bird is black except for white on belly, wing-tips, and shoulder blades.

An unmistakable member of the crow family, found in woods and open spaces, gardens and thickets. It will eat almost anything, but is notorious as a robber of the eggs of smaller birds.

None

46

CARRION CROW

18½in RESIDENT **47cm**

Entirely black with 'carr' call-note.

Feathered around base of bill unlike Rook. In flight tail end is square not slightly wedge-shaped as Rook.

A scavenger, feeding on carrion, small mammals and birds, frogs, insects, vegetable matter, grain, etc. Hence occurs almost everywhere – one of the most familiar birds.

Rook: pale grey, unfeathered area at base of bill (in adult only). **Jackdaw:** smaller; grey nape. **(Raven:** much larger 63.5cm (25″); 'Pruk' call.) **Hooded Crow:** sub-species replaces **Carrion Crow** in northern Britain; identical but for grey back and belly.

Black wings with a broad bright yellow band.

Adults have red, white and black markings on head, whilst head of juvenile is streaked brown. Rest of plumage, mainly brown with pale underparts and rump; again juvenile is streaked. All ages have white spots on wing and tail tips.

Gathered into flocks, Goldfinches feed mainly on thistle seeds in winter fields and gardens. Song is a liquid twitter and the flight is undulating.

Greenfinch: yellow patch on wing; yellow outer tail feathers; only likely to be confused at a distance. **(Siskin:** yellow on tail.)

Swallow-type bird with brown bar across breast.

Uniformly plain brown except for white underparts.

Smallest of the British Swallow-type birds, its method of feeding on the wing is typical, though its flight is less fluent. It nests in large colonies in burrows in sand cliffs or similar places.

House Martin: white rump. **Swallow:** long, forked tail; red face. **Swift:** scythe-shaped wings; no white underparts.

SEDGE WARBLER

13cm SUMMER VISITOR **5in**

Very prominent eye-stripe and black-streaked crown.

Small, plump warbler with streaked brown upper parts and creamy-coloured underparts. Plain rump and tail.

Inhabits reed-beds and other thicket and hedge areas near water. Song is a remarkably loud, unmelodic churring. When not singing it skulks nimbly through thick vegetation. During courtship gives parachute display.

(**Grasshopper Warbler:** less prominent eye-stripe; strange mechanical 'reeling' song.) Other **Warblers:** lack black streaks on crown; less prominent eye-stripes.

REED WARBLER
5in SUMMER VISITOR **13cm**

Unmarked (i.e. no eye-stripe, back or crown streaks).
Inhabits marshy areas. Note lookalikes below.

Warm rufous brown above with buff underparts and whitish
throat. Rounded tail. Dark legs.

Usually found in reed-beds or other vegetation near water.
Climbs restlessly in reeds where it builds remarkable suspended
nest. Song is a repetitive churring and often gives first warning
of bird's presence.

Female **Whitethroat:** prefers brambles, nettles and hedgerows.
Garden Warbler: plumper; woodland or heath habitat; square
tail. Other **Warblers:** Streaks, wing-bars or eye-stripes.

Male has head entirely black with white patch on side of neck and on wing. Female is brown with pale patch on wing. Consorts closely with male.

Male has brown, streaked back and white rump. Chestnut underparts. Colours are duller outside breeding season. Female is duller version of male but lacks head, neck and rump markings.

Inhabits heaths, commons, waste-ground and open farmland, especially if gorse growing. Typically perches on tops of gorse bushes and fence posts. Its name comes from the call which sounds like two stones clicking together.

Whinchat: similar to female only; mainly brown; white eye-stripe and cheek outline. **Redstart:** chestnut tail; male has white forehead. **Reed Bunting:** white outer tail feathers; male has white moustache. (**Pied Flycatcher:** white outer tail feathers; male black and white only.)

White eye-stripe and border around cheek. Female duller than male.

Back is brown and streaked. Underparts are buff. Sides of tail are white at the base. Only the male has the prominent white wing markings.

Prefers open country, grassland, heaths and gorse. Perches on prominent points with an upright posture, similar to its relative, the Stonechat. Flights between perches are short and rapid.

Stonechat: male has black head; both sexes lack white on tail feathers. **Sedge Warbler** and other **Warblers:** eye-stripes are not white; lack white tail feathers.

53

LINNET
13cm RESIDENT **5¼in**

♀

♂

Male has crimson crown and breast. Female has white patches on wing, and consorts closely with male.

Male has grey-brown head, brown back and buff underparts. Female is duller and streaked below. Both sexes and juveniles have white on the tail. Tail is markedly cleft.

Numerous on farmland and commons. The undulating flight and incessant twittering on the wing are good recognition features. Gregarious, they often associate with Greenfinches and Goldfinches.

(Redpoll: black spot under chin.) **(Twite:** almost no white on wings and tail; male has pink rump.) **Chaffinch:** two white wing-bars.

TREE SPARROW

5½in RESIDENT **14cm**

Chocolate-brown crown and black spot on cheek.

Brown-streaked back, pale grey cheeks and a small black bib. Pale grey underparts.

Unlike the House Sparrow, the Tree Sparrow mainly inhabits the countryside and is more wary of people.

House Sparrow: grey-brown; lacks cheek marking. **Dunnock:** different shape; slender bill; lacks pale cheeks.

White throat and outer tail feathers.

Male has grey cap. His pale underparts are often noticeably pinkish. Female has brown cap and pale underparts. Both sexes have brown back and long tail. White outer tail feathers are distinctive but rarely seen.

Prefers tangled undergrowth such as nettles, brambles and hedgerows. Brief, jerky flight often ends in a vertical drop into cover.

(**Lesser Whitethroat**: lacks rufous wings; dark 'mask' around eyes.) **Blackcap** (female): lacks white throat. **Reed Warbler**: similar to female Whitethroat but prefers wet habitats. **Garden Warbler**: grey-brown wings; grey throat. Other **Warblers** and **Flycatchers**: eye-stripes and/or wing-bars.

♀

♂

Black cap and white rump.

Male has grey back and bright pink breast. Female has grey nape, brown back and breast. Both sexes have black tail, black wings with faint white wing bar and a heavy bill. Juvenile as female but lacks black cap.

The bill is used for cracking seeds. Other foods include buds of fruit trees, making Bullfinches serious pests to fruit growers. Usually found in small woods and quiet gardens.

(**Brambling**: only similar in flight when white rump shows; lacks black cap; bright orange breast.) **Blackcap**: lacks white rump. **Marsh** and **Willow Tits**: lack white rump. **Redstart** (male): lacks white rump.

WHEATEAR

15cm SUMMER VISITOR **5¾in**

♀

♂

Black, inverted 'T' on a white rump and tail.

Male has black mask, white eyebrow and grey crown and back. Female has pale eye-stripe and brown upper parts. Both sexes are buff below and have brown-black wings.

Distinctive, trim bird with attractive markings and upright stance. Inhabits barren open places such as cliff-tops, moorland and bleak pasture. Bobs tail like Wagtail.

Redstart: lacks pied rump and tail markings. **Whinchat:** lacks pied rump and tail markings.

CHAFFINCH
5¾in RESIDENT **15cm**

♀

♂

Double white wing-bars and white outer tail feathers that are very conspicuous in flight.

Male has slate-blue crown, chestnut-brown back and pinkish face and breast. Female has greenish brown back, face and breast. Both sexes have green rump and blackish tail and wings.

Britain's commonest bird, numerous on farmland, hedgerows, woodland and gardens. Often forms large flocks in winter. Flight is markedly undulating.

(**Brambling:** white rump, orange breast.) **Bullfinch:** white rump; black cap. **Linnet:** lacks wing-bars. (**Twite:** lacks wing-bars.) **House Sparrow** (female): single wing-bar: lacks white on tail.

Heavy white moustache and white outer tail feathers.

Male has black head and throat and white collar. Female has brown head, pale throat and pale eye-stripe. Both sexes have brown, streaked backs and heavily streaked, pale underparts. Juveniles similar but yellower colouring.

Prefers watery areas such as reed-beds, marshes and wet meadows, but also occurs on heaths and cultivated fields. Usually perches on high vegetation.

(Female **Cirl Bunting**: yellower; lacks white moustache.) (**Corn Bunting**: lacks white outer tail feathers.) Female **Yellowhammer**: yellower; chestnut rump. **Meadow Pipit**: slimmer build; lacks moustache; beware similar call.

Similar to small Thrush with white outer tail feathers and weak 'tsip' call.

Brown above, streaked with darker markings and pale, streaked breast. Pinkish legs with long hind claws.

Abundant in open country, tolerating the harshest of conditions. Flight is hesitant. Wags tail when walking. Forms flocks in winter.

(**Tree Pipit:** yellower breast; more powerful 'teeze' call-note.)
Rock Pipit: larger; darker plumage; dark legs. **Skylark:** bulkier; crest.

Yellow head and chestnut rump.

Brown streaked back and brown tail with white outer feathers. Underparts yellowish and streaked. Females are generally duller than males.

Abundant in farmland, hedgerows and on commons. Large flocks may form in autumn on stubble fields. Distinctive call often rendered as 'little bit of bread and no cheese'.

(Cirl Bunting: olive brown rump.) **Reed Bunting** (female): lacks yellow colouring and chestnut rump.

BLUE-HEADED AND YELLOW WAGTAIL
6½in SUMMER VISITOR **17cm**

Blue-grey head and yellow throat (1), bright yellow face (2). Long tail which is repeatedly wagged.

Yellow breast, prominent eyebrow stripe, olive-green back and rump. Black tail with white outer feathers. The Blue-headed Wagtail **(1)** is a subspecies of the Yellow Wagtail **(2)**, which is restricted to Britain.

Prefer wet habitats such as water meadows, sewage farms, etc., in which to find insect food. Also on comparatively dry heathland. Typical Wagtail behaviour of bobbing and darting, and undulating flight.

Grey Wagtail: grey face and back.

Brilliant blue upper parts.

The underparts and cheeks are chestnut. The throat and sides of the neck are white. The dagger-shaped beak contrasts with the short, stumpy body.

May be seen around any fresh water location, and occasionally saltwater in winter. Habitually feeds on fish obtained by diving from a favourite perch. Also takes insects. Nests in burrows, usually in stream banks.

None.

Similar to small Thrush but has crest and white outer tail feathers.

Upper parts brown streaked with black. Pale underparts with black streaks on breast. Fairly long brown tail with white outer feathers.

Abundant in open country, the Skylark is most noted for its sustained song. It flies up to great heights to hang motionless while giving liquid, trilling outpourings. Bird may be so high as to be almost impossible to spot.

All **Pipits**: slimmer build; no crest.

♀

♂ ○

Grey face and extraordinarily long tail which is repeatedly wagged.

Grey back, greenish yellow rump, black tail with white outer feathers and yellow feathers under tail. Other underparts yellow in spring and summer, buff or white in autumn and winter. Male has white wing-bar and black bib. Female has white bib.

Almost invariably found by streams. Flicking of tail characteristic of all Wagtails, as are eccentric, dashing pursuit of insects and undulating flight.

Yellow Wagtail: olive green back.

WHITE AND PIED WAGTAIL

White, grey and black plumage, with long tail which is repeatedly wagged.

White face, dark crown, nape and bib, grey back, white underparts, and black tail with white outer feathers. European White Wagtail **(1)** is replaced in Britain by the black-backed (male only) subspecies **(2)**.

Inhabits any open country in which insects can be found. Undulating flight becomes rapidly erratic when chasing insects on the wing. On the ground, intersperses dashes after insects with pauses to wag tail.

(**Pied Flycatcher:** much shorter tail; very upright posture.)

Stocky brown and white bird.

Although apparently uniformly brown, head and belly are chestnut and the remainder is brown-black. Breast and throat are pure white.

Always near fast-flowing streams and rivers. Catches insects above and below the water surface. Walks along stream bed against current using wings to hold it down. Defends a stretch of stream against all-comers. 'Curtseys' repeatedly.

None.

Long forked tail and red face.

Blue-black back and pinkish underparts. Blue band across throat and blue cheeks border the red face. The tail feathers have white spots above and patches below.

Acrobatic flier, twisting and turning to catch insects often at very low level. Frequently nests inside farm buildings.

House Martin: white rump. **Sand Martin:** brown breast bar; white underparts. **Swift:** scythe-like wings; uniform brown plumage.

Light brown 'saddle' mark across neck.

Soft brown upper parts unusual for a wader. Pure white underparts and a streaked breast. In flight, shows conspicuous white wing-bars, and the white rump and outer tail feathers are divided by brown.

Low flight; stiff, bowed wings; and shallow rapid wing-beats are unique amongst waders, as is bobbing of tail like a Wagtail. Call is a clear 'twee-see-see'. Anywhere near water in summer; in autumn and winter on coasts and estuaries.

(**Wood Sandpiper**: lacks dark centre to tail; lacks wing-bar.)
(**Green Sandpiper**: very dark back; white rump; lacks wing-bar.)

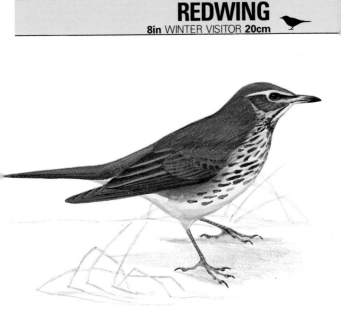

Bright red flanks and underwing.

Typical Thrush with speckled breast. Prominent white stripe over eye is often most easily seen feature.

Gregarious winter visitor to open areas and larger gardens seeking berries and fruit, worms and insects. Often flocks with Fieldfares.

Song Thrush: lacks eye-stripe; orange underwing. **Mistle Thrush:** larger; lacks eye-stripe; white underwing; white outer tail feathers. **Fieldfare:** grey head; brown back; grey rump; white underwing.

Grey head, brown back and grey rump.

A large thrush with typical speckled breast. Black tail, white underwing and golden throat and upper breast. Dark brown upper wing.

Extremely gregarious, often flocking with Redwings. Frequents the middle of fields, especially if damp.

Mistle Thrush: brown crown, back and rump. **Song Thrush:** smaller; orange underwing. **Redwing:** red underwing; prominent eye-stripe.

Zig-zag flight and 'scaap' alarm-call when flushed.

Rich brown back streaked with buff and black. White belly. Breast and flanks buff with dark markings. Crown black with buff streak. Tail rich brown barred with black. Long, straight bill roughly one quarter of the body-length.

Inhabits most wet habitats from bogs to salt marshes. Well camouflaged and secretive, usually seen only when flushed. In spring, conspicuous display flight in which bird dives through air, vibrating tail feathers making 'drumming' sound.

(**Jack Snipe**: similar; smaller; flushes silently with shorter, more direct flight.) (**Woodcock**: larger; not gregarious; inhabits woodland.)

LITTLE GREBE (or DABCHICK)
27cm RESIDENT **10½in**

Small size and distinctive shape, and (in summer) yellowish base to bill.

Summer: dark brown with chestnut cheeks and throat. Tail is blunt-ended and often fluffed. Winter: plumage paler; chestnut turns to buff; flanks fade to buff.

Inhabits any stretch of quiet water. Though common, habits are skulking and may be difficult to see for any length of time. Dives frequently.

(**Black-necked Grebe:** summer – drooping golden ear tufts; winter – black and grey neck; upturned bill.)

SPARROWHAWK

11-15in RESIDENT **28-38cm**

Broad, round-tipped wings and barred underparts.

Male has blue-grey upper parts, brick-red underparts. Smaller (28cm/11in) than female (38cm/15in). Female has brown upper parts with strongly barred tail. Pale underparts. White eyebrow. Both sexes have yellow legs.

Always close to woodland preferring mixed country with woods and open farmland. Small birds and sometimes mammals taken from swift, low flight, usually shooting out from behind cover of a hedge, etc. Soars but does not hover.

Buzzards (and **Eagle**): much larger; short tails. **Kestrel** (and all **Falcons**): pointed wings. **Kestrels**: hover. (**Harriers**: long narrow wings.) (**Kites**: forked tails.)

Orange-red face and pale-grey neck and breast.

Typical game bird. Has round, chicken-like shape. The back, upper wing, rump and inner tail are all brown with buff streaks. Outer tail and horseshoe-shape patch on belly are chestnut. Flanks barred chestnut. Underparts pale grey.

Very shy bird usually seen in small flocks (coveys) on cultivated land and occasionally on heaths and moors. Takes flight on whirring wings at the least disturbance. Lays enormous clutches, up to 20 eggs, in hedgerows.

Red-legged Partridge: similar at a distance; white face; black 'necklace'. **Red Grouse:** entirely red-brown.

Long crest and laboured flapping flight on broad, round-tipped wings.

Though appears black and white at a distance, is actually mainly dark green and white. Orange under the tail.

Eerie 'peewit' call gives bird its country name. Calls often from tumbling display flight. Flocks in winter on farmland and other open ground. A member of the Plover family. Like other waders favours marshy land, especially when breeding.

None.

White stripe on flank.

Though often appearing black, plumage is dark brown. Red shield above bill and white outer tail feathers also very distinctive.

Favours variety of fresh water habitats from small ponds to large reservoirs. Easily disturbed, displays alarm by flicking tail to display white outer feathers.

Coot: white shield above; lacks stripes on flank.

STOCK DOVE

13in RESIDENT **33cm**

Upper wing has black borders, lower wing does not.

Lacks any white markings. Plumage generally drab grey, but for black tip to tail, green patch on neck and pink breast.

Inhabits woods and open country. Flight is fast and direct. Often flocks on farmland.

Feral Pigeon: usually lacks pink breast; black border below wing, not above. **Wood Pigeon:** white flashes on wing. **Collared Dove:** zig-zag black collar. **(Turtle Dove:** pied markings on neck.)

KESTREL
33-36cm RESIDENT **13-14in**

♀

♂

Hovers for long periods.

Pointed wings and long thin tail of a Falcon. Male has blue-grey head, rump and tail. Back and inner wing rufous, with black spots. Outer wing and tail tip black. Female has upper parts rufous, barred with black. Tail tip black.

Widely distributed in all types of country. Has successfully adapted to towns and particularly to motorway verges.

All **Hawks**: broad, round-tipped wings. **Buzzard** (and **Eagle**): much larger. (**Harriers**: much larger.) (**Kites**: forked tails.) (Other **Falcons** do not hover.)

80

Black band passing through eye and around neck.

Typical game bird with plump, chicken-like shape. White face. Upper parts plain brown and outer tail chestnut. Buff belly. Breast and most of underwing grey. Flanks barred black, white and deep red. Legs and bill red.

Like Partridge, generally in small flocks (coveys) on agricultural land, but also on heaths and even coastal dunes. Very wary, will run off rather than fly. Lays up to 16 eggs in nest hollow scraped under cover.

Partridge: similar at a distance; orange face; grey neck; no black stripe on grey neck; horseshoe on belly. **Red Grouse:** entirely red-brown.

BARN OWL
34cm RESIDENT **13½in**

Owl with unmarked, white underparts.

Beautiful orange and buff mottled upper parts contrasting with white, heart-shaped face.

Often nests and roosts in rural buildings. Otherwise favours woodland and marshy places. Mainly nocturnal, most often seen at twilight. Flight is buoyant and unhurried, with periodic short glides.

All other **Owls**: dark or streaked underparts.

Chicken-shaped moorland bird with white-feathered feet.

Colour varies from all-white plumage of Willow Grouse (1), through white and red-brown summer plumage to the fully red-brown Red Grouse (2). Males show a red wattle above the eye.

Restricted to Northern Europe, except for infrequent visitors, these species favour heather moorland, lowland heaths and bogs. Flight is strong and low, swift wingbeats alternating with long glides.

Partridge: orange-red face; grey neck. **Red-legged Partridge:** white face; black stripe across chest.

Smallest duck with green and black speculum; white wing-bars, prominent before speculum, obscure behind.

Male has chestnut head. Green patch around eye. Grey back, wings and flanks. Spotted, buff breast. Yellow triangle under tail. At rest, horizontal white stripe above wing. Female is buff-brown. Underparts paler and heavily spotted.

Fast fliers on rapid wing-beats, often in large flocks which twist and turn in flight. Favour wet, marshy areas in the breeding season, and reservoirs, lakes and sewage farms at other times.

None.

White shield over bill.

Entirely black except for greenish legs and lobe-webbed feet.

More aquatic than the Moorhen, Coots favour wide stretches of open water. Gregarious birds, they often flock in winter on lakes and gravel pits.

Moorhen: white stripes on flank; red shield above bill.

85

The only duck with a crest (more prominent in male).

Male is all black except for pure white flanks. Female plumage is duller but reminiscent of male, occasionally with small white mark at base of bill. Both sexes have white wing-bar, prominent when in flight.

Numerous freshwater diving duck. Often flocks with other ducks in winter on ponds, reservoirs, etc.

None.

Male has chestnut head, black breast and bluish band around bill. Female markings are reminiscent of male but duller. Bluish band around bill.

Remainder of bill black. Lack of distinct wing markings (nondescript grey bar only). (Male) light grey back and flanks, black rump and under-tail. (Female) brown but reminiscent of male. Buff band around the cheeks.

Inhabits slow-moving waterways, preferring lakes, reservoirs, etc. A diving duck which runs across the water when taking off.

(Wigeon: buff crown; lacks black breast.) Other female Ducks: lack black bill with blue band.

87

Entirely black with pale grey face.

Pale face distinguishes the Rook from the Carrion Crow (except in immatures). Other features include more slender bill, more upright stance, shaggy thigh feathers and wedge-shaped tail in flight.

Normally inhabits agricultural land but also moorland and other open country. Nests in large colonies called rookeries.

Carrion Crow: black face; 'carr' call-note. **Jackdaw:** grey nape; smaller. **(Raven:** huge; 'pruk' call-note.)

White neck and black ear tufts (tufts small in winter).

Long pointed bill, long neck, grey back and virtually no tail. Summer: chestnut frills develop below and behind cheeks. Ear tufts enlarge. Winter: no frills, tufts smaller and bill noticeably pinkish.

Inhabits large areas of water such as reservoirs, gravel pits, and lakes. Builds nest in vegetation at water's edge.

None.

SHOVELER
51cm RESIDENT **20in**

♀

♂

Distinctive spatulate bill. Pale blue forewing and green speculum with white wing-bar.

Male has green head, white breast, scapulars (outer back) and tip of tail. Chestnut flanks and belly. Centre of back dark brown. Black rump and under-tail. Female is a uniformly mottled brown.

Feeds by dabbling, swimming rapidly with head held low filtering plant food from water surface. When disturbed, rises vertically from the water.

Shelduck: chestnut band across chest; normal bill shape. All other **Ducks:** lack spatulate bill.

Brown tail with narrow bars.

Soars effortlessly on straight wings. Tail broad and rounded when fanned. Neck very short. Wing tips rounded with finger-like tips. Brown back, paler below, streaked.

Frequents secluded are s in hill country and moorland in western England, Wales, and Scotland. May perch on telegraph poles, fences and so on.

(**Golden Eagle:** neck and head project further; larger – 30-34in/76-86cm; north Scotland only.) (**Rough-legged Buzzard:** white tail with black band at tip: migratory through north Scotland, east coast of England.) (**Honey Buzzard:** brown tail with black tip; summer visitor.)

PHEASANT
53-89cm RESIDENT **21-35in**

Extremely long tail

Male has green head with red wattled face. White collar.
Golden-brown body, breast and flanks with black crescent
markings. Female is uniform buff-brown, paler below. In both
sexes plumage is variable. Long tail is barred.

Commonest on cultivated farmland, also in woods and open
country.

None

MALLARD
23in RESIDENT **58cm**

Purple speculum (band of colour on inner wing), bordered with white.

Male has yellow bill, glossy green head and upper neck. White collar, brown breast, grey-brown back and wings. Distinctive curly tail feathers. Female has brown bill. All plumage except speculum is a mixture of browns, buffs and black.

Commonest duck in Europe. Surface-feeding on any slow moving water body. Much domesticated, numerous varieties include the pure white Aylesbury. When bred with the wild Mallard mixed offspring are produced.

(**Red-breasted Merganser:** white speculum; crest.) **Shoveler:** distinctive spatulate bill. All other **Ducks:** lack purple speculum.

93

GREY HERON
90cm RESIDENT **35in**

Grey wings and back.

Long bill, neck and legs. Black eye-stripe runs into black crest. Black-tipped wings. Flies with even, leisurely wing-beats, neck folded back between shoulders and legs trailing.

Always near water whether ditches, ponds, rivers or lakes, where it stands motionless waiting to lunge at passing fish. Widespread.

None.

Goose with white patch on face and brown back.

Black head and neck. Brown wings and belly. White breast and rump. Black tail.

An introduced bird, widely distributed though still low in numbers. Its distinctive markings and liking for small ponds make it a familiar sight. In winter they may gather in large numbers to graze on grassland and marshes.

(Barnacle Goose: face entirely white; back grey.) **(Brent Goose:** far smaller; head dark; white patch halfway down neck.) (Other **Geese:** lack white on face.)

MUTE SWAN
152cm RESIDENT **60in**

Huge white bird with an orange-red bill.

Distinctive black knob at base of bill, larger in male. Black legs. Body, excluding neck, is about 76cm (30in).

Common on slow moving, open water. Graceful S-shape of neck contrasts with other, rarer swans. In flight, noisy throbbing wing-beats may be heard over long distances.

(**Bewick's Swan:** black and yellow bill; neck held more vertical.)

Similar to small Thrush. Grey outer tail feathers. Occurs only on rocky coastlines.

Dark brown with darker streaks above. Paler breast with dark streaks. Very dark legs.

Inhabits rocky coastlines seeking insects on exposed seaweed. Water Pipits are a different race of this species – much less common, they prefer mountain slope habitats.

Meadow Pipit: paler; white outer tail feathers; pale legs. (**Tree Pipit:** yellower breast; 'teeze' call.) **Skylark:** bulkier; crest on head.

DUNLIN

17-19cm RESIDENT **7-7½in**

In summer, black belly and longish, slightly downcurved bill. In winter, grey-brown back and longish, slightly downcurved bill.

In summer, chestnut brown upper parts with black markings. In winter, grey-brown upper parts. Pale grey breast streaks on otherwise white underparts. At all times, in flight, clear wing-bar and white rump divided by black.

Britain's commonest wader. Its striking mannerisms include a 'stitching' feeding motion as it probes the mud. Rather round-shouldered in appearance. Highly gregarious.

(**Golden Plover** and **Grey Plover:** (summer) black belly extends to face; short straight bill.) (**Sanderling:** (summer): no black belly; short straight bill.) **Knot:** (summer): lacks black belly; larger; stockier; straight bill. (**Little Stint:** tiny; V-mark on back.)

RINGED PLOVER
7½in RESIDENT **19cm**

Black collar beneath white face with black eye-stripe and band on forehead.

Small, stout bird, brown above and white below. In flight conspicuous white wing-bar on upper wing and brown back extends to divide white rump. Orange-yellow legs. Bill orange at base and black at tip.

One of Britain's commonest waders, feeding along shore-line on coasts and estuaries. Flight is low and rapid. Often associates with Dunlin.

(**Little Ringed Plover:** lacks white wing-bar; extra line on crown.) **Turnstone:** different face pattern; white tail and rump in flight.

'Tortoiseshell' back plumage and a dark breastband.

Upper parts darken in winter to a mottled brown. A plump little bird with bright orange legs and short bill. In flight entire back and wings distinctively pied.

Entirely coastal, feeding on or around seashores and rocks. Jerky actions and short skittering runs.

Knot (and **Sanderling** and **Purple Sandpiper**) (winter only) lack distinct breast band. **Ringed Plover**: black collar beneath white face with black eye-stripe and band on forehead.

Extremely gregarious. Stout, short-legged wader with scaly grey markings on back. In summer has brown head and underparts.

Larger and stockier than Dunlin. Grey back and white underparts with grey marked flanks and breast. Pale wing-bar visible in flight, as is pale rump and tail. Bill is straight and short.

Mainly coastal and on estuaries feeding in enormous flocks. Call-note is 'nut' and flight-call 'twit-it'. *Also a passage migrant.

(Grey Plover: (summer) black underparts; (winter) black 'armpits'.) **Dunlin:** smaller; decurved bill; white rump divided with black. **(Sanderling:** smaller; dark-legged; very white belly.) **Turnstone:** (winter only) distinct breast band.

REDSHANK
28cm RESIDENT **11in**

In flight, white rump and strips on trailing edge of wings form characteristic triple pattern.

One of Britain's commonest waders. Orange-red legs. Orange-red bill, tipped with black. Brown back. Pale underparts, breast and head all streaked with brown.

Very nervous bird, easily disturbed. Flies off after a couple of dips of the head and a penetrating 'tleu-hu-hu' alarm call.

(**Greenshank:** no white on wings in flight; greenish legs.)
(**Spotted Redshank:** no white on wings; confusion only likely in winter plumage.) (**Ruff:** faint wing-bar; white rump divided; shorter bill). **Oystercatcher:** pied plumage, though larger white areas on wings and rump similar.

Extraordinary triangular bill, multi-coloured in summer.

Black crown, nape, back and wings. White underparts, off-white face and bright orange feet.

Extremely fast, 'whirring' wing-beats and splayed feet on landing typical of all auks. Nests in burrows on cliff faces and tops.

None.

COMMON TERN
33-36cm SUMMER VISITOR **13-14in**

Red bill with black tip in adult.

Resembles a slender gull with forked tail and buoyant flight. Cap
only is black. Grey above and white below with thin dark strip
on leading edge of outer wing. Good light shows transparent
panel on inner primaries.

Visits Britain March-November. Catches fish by diving from a
hovering position. Occurs coastally and at water bodies inland.

Arctic Tern: blood-red bill; short legs. **(Little Tern:** smaller;
yellow bill.) **(Sandwich Tern:** black bill with yellow tip; crest on
head.) **Black-headed Gull:** chocolate-brown head (summer).

Tern with blood-red bill in adult.

Resembles a slender gull with forked tail and buoyant flight. Cap only is black. Grey above and white below with white rump. In good light all primaries appear transparent. At rest, noticeably short-legged.

Visits Britain March-September. Catches fish by diving from a hover. Usually coastal.

Common Tern: red bill has black tip. **(Little Tern:** smaller; yellow bill.) **(Sandwich Tern:** black bill with yellow tip; crest on head.) **Black-headed Gull:** chocolate-brown head (summer).

KITTIWAKE
41cm RESIDENT **16in**

Black legs and all-black wing-tips.

White except for grey back and upper wings and black wing-tips. Yellow bill. Juveniles have dark spot on ear, black collar, black 'W' mark on back and wings and black end to tail.

Follows ships with typical buoyant flight. Feeds entirely at sea. 'Kitti-waake' call gives bird its name.

Common Gull: yellow legs: black wing-tips tipped with white. **Black-headed Gull:** red legs; white leading edge to wing; chocolate-brown head in summer.

Thick black bill marked with white vertical stripe.

Upper parts and head black. Underparts white. Black feet.

A thick-set auk with typical maritime habits, nesting in cliff-ledge colonies, frequently in association with Guillemots. Flight over sea is low on rapid wing-beats.

Guillemot: sleeker; pointed bill; upper parts very dark brown.

107

GUILLEMOT

42cm RESIDENT **16½in**

Uniform dark-brown upper parts and slender pointed bill.

Underparts white, feet brown. In winter black cheeks and throat turn white. 'Bridled' form (in limited numbers of the population in any area) has white line around eye and backwards over the ear.

A sleek and slender auk. Thoroughly maritime with low flight on rapidly beating wings. Nests on cliff-ledge colonies, frequently in association with Razorbills.

Razorbill: thick black bill with vertical white stripe.

OYSTERCATCHER

17in RESIDENT **43cm**

Pied plumage and long, straight orange-red bill.

Glossy, black head, throat, back and wings contrast with a white wing-bar, lower breast, belly and rump. Long legs are pink and eyes are red.

A large, common, distinctive wader. Seen singly or in large flocks on seashores, estuaries and other wet areas – sometimes miles inland. A shy bird, it is easily startled into flight giving its shrill piping call.

(**Avocet:** thin upward-curving black bill.) **Redshank:** smaller; mainly brown plumage; similar white areas on wings and rump.

FULMAR
47cm RESIDENT **18½in**

Bull-necked with long wings held straight and stiff in flight.

Tube-nosed. Grey above, without any black on wings and white below.

Gull-like in appearance but masterful flight quite distinct. Clumsy on land, it has difficulty in landing and taking off. Deters intruders by spitting foul-smelling stomach-oils.

Herring Gull and **Common Gull**: black tips to wings.

Dark-grey back and yellow legs.

White except for dark grey upper wings. In winter neck is often streaked and legs may fade to grey or even pinkish-grey. Red spot on bill. Juveniles and immatures mottled brown above.

Basically coastal, but may venture inland, especially when migrating, or in winter when resident population widens area of search for food.

Great Black-backed Gull: very much larger and bulkier; black back; legs always flesh-coloured. **Herring Gull:** light-grey back and wings; flesh-coloured legs. **Common Gull:** smaller and more slender; light grey back and wings; no red bill spot.

CURLEW
53-58cm RESIDENT **21-23in**

Extremely long downward-curved bill. No bold stripes on crown.

Britain's largest wader. Streaky brown plumage becomes considerably paler towards white belly and rump. Tail is barred brown. Legs are long and grey-green.

Although usually thought of as estuarine, during the breeding season it often inhabits marshy fields and so on. It is gregarious and easily disturbed. Beautiful call is an eerie series of bubbling notes.

None.

Grey back and flesh-coloured legs.

White except for grey upper wings and black wing-ends. Wing-tips are pure white. In winter the neck is streaked. Red spot on bill. Juveniles and immatures are mottled brown above.

Found coastally and inland. A raucous scavenger, frequent at rubbish tips.

Common Gull: smaller and slimmer; yellow legs; no red spot on bill. **Lesser Black-backed Gull:** dark grey back and wings; yellow legs. **Black-headed Gull** (winter only): dark ear-spot; red or deep orange legs; red bill; white leading edge to wings. **Fulmar:** straight wings; no black wing-tips.

Black and white with chestnut band around body.

Large goose-shaped duck with a red bill and pink feet. 'Black' plumage is actually very dark green and wing has a bright green speculum. Bill of male has a red knob.

Estuarine and coastal. General behaviour rather goose-like. Nests in burrows.

Shoveler: extraordinary spatulate bill.

Black back and flesh-coloured legs.

White apart from black upper wing. A very large robust gull with a red spot on bill. Neck may be streaked in winter. Juveniles and immatures are mottled brown above.

Basically coastal, it rarely ventures inland in winter though estuaries are a favourite haunt. May kill small animals and birds as well as being a scavenger.

Lesser Black-backed Gull: notably smaller and slimmer; dark grey back and wings; yellow legs. **Herring Gull:** notably smaller and slimmer, light grey back and wings.

CORMORANT
91cm RESIDENT **36in**

Black seabird with white cheeks.

Predominantly blackish all over. White cheeks extend to the chin. White patches on thighs in breeding season.

Almost entirely coastal, it is often seen flying low over the water with a fast direct flight. At rest it perches upright, often with its wings held out to dry.

(**Shag:** bottle-green; crested; lacks white markings.) **Canada Goose:** brown wings and back.

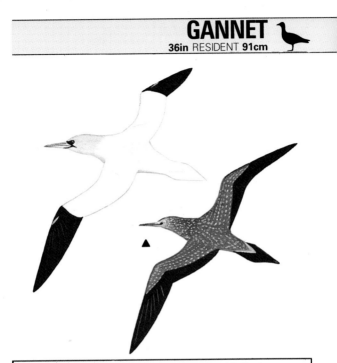

Massive wingspan approaching two metres (six feet).

The body is distinctly cigar-shaped and the wings long and narrow. Adults have white wings and body, black wing-tips and golden-yellow head. Immatures are speckled black, brown and white in varying degrees.

Flies low over sea in leisurely manner. When feeding on fish performs spectacular dives, often from considerable heights. Wings folded backwards on instant of entry to the water.

None.

Firecrest   **9 cm/3½ in**

Crested Tit   **11 cm/4½ in**

Siskin   **11 cm/4½ in**

Little Stint   **13 cm/5 in**

Grasshopper Warbler   **13 cm 5 in**

Dartford Warbler   **13 cm/5 in**

Wood Warbler   **13 cm/5 in**

Pied Flycatcher   **13 cm/5 in**

Cetti's Warbler   **14 cm/5½ in**

Lesser Whitethroat **14 cm/5½ in**

Less Common Species

Black Redstart   **14 cm/5½ in**

Twite   **14 cm/5½ in**

Redpoll   **14 cm/5½ in**

Little Ringed Plover   **15 cm/6 in**

Lesser Spotted Woodpecker
15 cm/6 in

Tree Pipit   **15 cm/6 in**

Brambling   **15 cm/6 in**

Nightingale   **17 cm/6½ in**

Bearded Tit   **17 cm/6½ in**

Cirl Bunting   **17 cm/6½ in**

119

Snow Bunting   **17 cm/6½ in**

Crossbill   **17 cm/6½ in**

Waxwing   **18 cm/7 in**

Corn Bunting   **18 cm/7 in**

Jack Snipe   **19 cm/7½ in**

Sanderling   **20 cm/8 in**

Wood Sandpiper   **20 cm/8 in**

Purple Sandpiper   **21 cm/8½ in**

Ruff   **22-30 cm/8½-12 in**

Little Owl   **22 cm/8½ in**

Green Sandpiper   **23 cm/9 in**

Black Tern   **24 cm/9½ in**

Little Tern   **24 cm/9½ in**

Great Grey Shrike   **24 cm/9½ in**

Ring Ouzel   **24 cm/9½ in**

Merlin   **27-33 cm/10½-13 in**

Turtle Dove   **27 cm/10½ in**

Nightjar   **27 cm/10½ in**

Water Rail   **28 cm/11 in**

Golden Plover   **28 cm/11 in**

Grey Plover   **28 cm/11 in**

Bee-Eater   **28 cm/11 in**

Hoopoe   **28 cm/11 in**

Black-necked Grebe **30 cm/12 in**

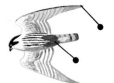

Hobby   **30-36 cm/12-14 in**

Spotted Redshank   **30 cm/12 in**

Greenshank   **31 cm/12 in**

Cuckoo   **33 cm/13 in**

Woodcock   **34 cm/13½ in**

Manx Shearwater   **35 cm/14 in**

122

Less Common Species

Peregrine   **38-48 cm/15-19 in**

Bar-tailed Godwit   **38 cm/15 in**

Short-eared Owl   **38 cm/15 in**

Black-tailed Godwit
39 cm/15½ in

Sandwich Tern   **41 cm/16 in**

Hen Harrier   **43-51 cm/17-20 in**

Avocet   **43 cm/17 in**

Wigeon   **46 cm/18 in**

Arctic Skua   **46 cm/18 in**

Common Scoter   **48 cm/19 in**

123

Marsh Harrier
**48-56 cm
19-22 in**

Gadwall
51 cm/20 in

Osprey
51-58 cm/20-23 in

Honey Buzzard
**51-58 cm
20-23 in**

Rough-legged Buzzard
51-56 cm/20-22 in

Brent Goose
56-61 cm/22-24 in

Pintail
55-66 cm/22-26 in

Barnacle Goose
**58-69 cm
23-27 in**

Eider
58 cm/23 in

Red-breasted Merganser
58 cm/23 in

124

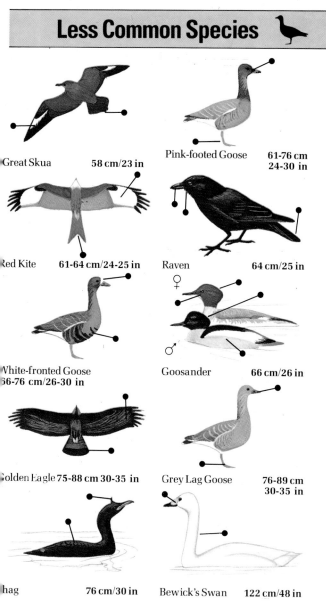

Great Skua   **58 cm/23 in**

Pink-footed Goose   **61-76 cm 24-30 in**

Red Kite   **61-64 cm/24-25 in**

Raven   **64 cm/25 in**

White-fronted Goose 66-76 cm/26-30 in

♀
♂
Goosander   **66 cm/26 in**

Golden Eagle **75-88 cm 30-35 in**

Grey Lag Goose   **76-89 cm 30-35 in**

Shag   **76 cm/30 in**

Bewick's Swan   **122 cm/48 in**

125

Index and check-list

Keep a record of your sightings by inserting a tick in the box.

FURTHER READING

A Field Guide to the Birds of Great Britain and Europe,
  Peterson, Mountford and Hollom. Collins, London, 1954.
*The Birds of Britain and Europe with North Africa and the
  Middle East.* Collins, London, 1972.
The Mitchell Beazley Birdwatchers' Pocket Guide, Peter
  Hayman, Mitchell Beazley, London, 1979.
The Penguin Lars Johnsson Series, Lars Johnsson. Penguin,
  London, 1978/79.
The RSPB Guide to British Birds, David Saunders. Hamlyn,
  London, 1975.